Affiliate Marketing

Unleash The Potential Of Affiliate Marketing To Increase Your Earnings

(Proven Free Traffic Strategies For Success In Affiliate Marketing)

Thomas Andreoli

TABLE OF CONTENT

Introduction 1

Chapter 1: Copywriting Methodology 8

Chapter 2: An Unshakeable Marketing Strategy 16

Chapter 3: Selecting Superior Affiliate Products 24

Chapter 4: Launching And Enhancing Your Website's Search Engine Visibility 31

Chapter 5: Publish Your Post 42

Chapter 6: How Do You Get Individuals To Speak? 54

Chapter 7: Developing Professionalism 68

Chapter 8: How To Select Affiliate Products Intelligently 88

Chapter 9: Optimize Your Affiliate Links In Order To Gain More Clicks 118

Chapter 10: The Positives Of Drop Shipping 121

Chapter 11: How To Develop An Entrepreneurial Mindset 130

Chapter 12: Covers Audience Growth And Product Marketing 139

Chapter 13: Utilizing And Various Other Platforms For Direct Sales 149

Chapter 14: Choosing The Appropriate Affiliate Program 161

Conclusion: 168

Introduction

With the internet at your disposal, it is no longer difficult to operate an affiliate marketing company. In the past, consumers were required to use the telephone and other informational channels to obtain the most up-to-date information about their program's progress; however, this is no longer the case.

Given the available technology and assuming that they work from home, an affiliate's typical day may therefore resemble the following:

She examines the network for the most recent network updates after waking up, eating breakfast, and turning on her computer. The marketer's perspective may necessitate the collection of updated data and statistics.

The affiliate program should be submitted to directories that list affiliate programs once it has been completed. These directories serve as a means of recruitment for your affiliate program. A trustworthy technique of promoting the affiliate program.

It is time to accurately and fairly monitor the sales your affiliates generate. Orders are available via phone and mail.

Determine whether they are prospective new consumers. Keeping note of the contact information of potential sources for future use.

It is necessary to organize many resources. Since the marketer is aware that distributing advertisements, banners, buttons, and sample recommendations can increase sales, they do so.

It is optimal to remain accessible and visible.

It was communicated to the affiliate marketer that queries from site visitors needed to be answered. It must be completed immediately. Unanswered correspondence is the number one turnoff for clients.

If the Affiliate intended to demonstrate its effectiveness and efficiency, it would be necessary to give more weight to inquiries. The majority of customers are not the most patient individuals, and no one enjoys being disregarded. A concise response that appears professional and approachable.

While completing all required tasks, the marketer connects to a discussion room to interact with other affiliates and program members. Here, they can discuss the most effective methods to market their products.

Learning is an ongoing process, and there are things to learn. The exchange of advice can be an effective means of providing assistance. The discussion that is presently taking place may attract additional participants. It is acceptable to make assumptions about prospective clients.

Since newsletters and e-zines were updated a few days ago, the affiliate marketer should determine if there have been any recent market developments. This will be addressed in the marketer's magazine, which will be distributed to both current and prospective customers.

The same periodicals are essential for staying abreast of newly introduced products. The marketer has established a promotion and campaign.

It is time to express gratitude to all those who assisted the marketer in increasing sales through promotions. There is no greater way to express gratitude to the people, places, and systems responsible for making everything possible.

This will undoubtedly be published in the newsletters. It contains some of the most significant works of ancient literature.

There is still time for the marketer to provide guidance to those seeking reputable suppliers of the offered products. There is time to share success tips with other aspiring affiliate marketers on a website with many of them.

Time is fleeting. He skipped lunch but is pleased with his accomplishments. Time for bed...

Therefore, it is conceivable that this will not be completed in a single day. However, this gives you an indication of an affiliate marketer's typical marketing day.

Is that success' specter, or what?

Chapter 1: Copywriting Methodology

With the aid of a copywriting formula, you can write your copy more quickly and with a higher probability of success. Be aware that various groups, content types, and writing styles require different formulas. Criteria for business copywriting formula; 1. Simple to memorize and master

2. able to assist novice and seasoned copywriters in producing effective copy swiftly

3. Possess a proven track record of success, in some instances spanning decades. Below are the most frequently used copywriting formulas:

First copywriting formula: AIDA

This is one of the earliest formulas that continues to function effectively. It has been utilized in direct mail, radio, television, sales pages, landing pages, BlogSpot, and social media advertisements, etc.

Attention: Disrupt the reader's routine; construct attention-getting phrases that stand out among other competitor's messages. Attractiveness: Information that is interesting and new and appeals to the reader Engage their heart so that they desire what you are offering.

Request that they take the next step.

Second copywriting formula: AIDCA

Very similar to the first formula, with the addition of a C, which stands for ;

Create in your reader the desire and conviction to use your solution.

Formula 3 for writing copy: The 4Cs Understand your audience and your objectives; make your writing more comprehensible by using small words, brief sentences, a header, and bullet points. Have information communicated in as few words as feasible. Copy must also be engaging enough for the target audience to actually read it.

The secret is to focus on the requirements of the reader. Problems and desires.

Credible: Write in such a way that the promises you are making can be trusted. Provide customer testimonials to address the skepticism of your audience.

Fourth copywriting formula: PAS Dan Kennedy referred to PAS as the most trustworthy sales formula ever created. Present the problem your prospect is experiencing. Agitation: Poke at the problem until a desire to find a solution emerges. Present your solution to the difficult issue.

The fifth copywriting formula is narrative.

These formulas for storytelling will be unique, attention-grabbing, and engaging to the audience. It can be composed of the following three components:

Star: The protagonist of your story

The narrative itself

How the protagonist triumphs in the end The sixth copywriting formula is objection management.

Your audience might be dubious. Selling involves overcoming objections. If your copy can overcome these common objections, you have a good chance of convincing your audience to act at the conclusion.

I do not have sufficient funds.

2. I lack sufficient leisure.

It does not work for me

4. I don't believe you

5. I do not require it

These copywriting formulas provide a useful guide, particularly for getting started fast with copywriting. After becoming a frequent writer, you may no longer need to refer to these formulas. Instead of simply reading this, take out your notebook and begin practicing the formulas.

Easy Affiliate Guide

Here's the link that will teach you everything you need to know or do to begin earning money through affiliate marketing.

14. Track your progress

As an affiliate marketer, it is essential to continually monitor your results in order to optimize your campaigns and maximize your earnings potential. You can monitor a variety of different metrics, the most important of which are conversion rate, click-through rate, and average order value.

In order to monitor your results, you must add tracking codes to your affiliate links. These codes will enable you to determine how many individuals clicked on your link and how many of those clicks led to a sale. Then, you can use this information to determine your conversion rate and click-through rate.

Additionally, it is essential to monitor your average order value, as this will give you an indication of how much revenue your affiliate marketing is generating. Simply divide your total affiliate earnings by the number of sales you generated to accomplish this.

Regularly monitoring your results will help you identify areas in which you can enhance your affiliate marketing efforts. By monitoring your progress and making adjustments as necessary, you can ensure that your affiliate campaigns generate the highest possible earnings.

- Monitoring and Conversion

If you want to be a successful affiliate marketer, you'll need additional tools to monitor the effectiveness of your advertisements and convert your audience. Google Analytics must be installed on every site. It is efficacious and cost-free. Google is ultimately the most popular search engine. That implies you must adhere to their recommendations.

prettylinks.com is a great option for link monitoring. Your website may be configured so that the affiliate link is added automatically whenever you mention a particular term. It's an excellent method for automating your ideas and tracking interactions and conversions.

Chapter 2: An Unshakeable Marketing Strategy

Now that you comprehend the various components of social media marketing, it is time to develop a rock-solid marketing strategy! In this chapter, we will construct a marketing plan that incorporates all the moving parts of social media marketing so that you can make sense of what you have learned and build a successful strategy. By the end of this chapter, you will understand precisely what must be done to achieve social media success.

Step 1: Conceptualize Your Foundation

The first stage in constructing a rock-solid marketing strategy is determining the foundation. To accomplish this, return to the chapter on platforms and select the one that makes the most sense for your company. Start by selecting a platform based on the average age of users for that platform. Then, narrow it down based on the type of content that is most likely to be effective for your company. For instance, if you are a creative, a photo-based platform is likely to perform exceptionally well for you. A text-based or video-based platform is likely to perform better for professionals.

Understand Your Sales Funnel

Now, you need to identify your unique sales funnel stages. This is straightforward to restrict. Consider first why people would be interested in your business. What do you do that distinguishes you and makes you interesting? This will serve as the foundation for your content's appeal. Next, consider why people would choose your company over others. Why are you more approachable than your rival? Consider why people would want to purchase from your company. Which product do they require the most, and why? Your sales funnel will be based on the answers to these three queries.

Step 3: Research Appealing Content Techniques

As you develop your strategy, you must investigate the types of appealing content that are appropriate for your niche and your goals. Examine the content of your competitors and how they are expanding their audiences in order to determine what is appealing. What kind of content do they utilize? Exists a correlation between the content categories utilized by various competitors? How can you employ your unique factors of likeability to these strategies?

What Works plus Your Unique Likeability Factors = Your Likable Content Strategy

Research relationship-building content strategies in the fourth step.

Examine how your competitors cultivate relationships with their audience as part of your research. What type of content are they posting, what key points are they highlighting, and how are they utilizing this to develop relationships with their audience? How do they interact with their audience when it interacts with them? What can you do to tailor this strategy to your brand's personality?

What Works Plus Your Unique Personality Equals Your Relationship-Building Strategy

Step 5 is to investigate sales content strategies

Finally, investigate how your competitors sell their products and services. What sort of content do they use to share information about their products? What are they saying, and what calls-to-action (CTAs) are they using to motivate their audience to purchase? How can this be applied to your own offers?

What Works plus Your Unique Offers = Sales Content Strategy is your sales content formula.

Create your content calendar as the sixth step

After determining which types of content will perform best, you must strategize your content. In the following chapter, I will demonstrate how to do this by creating specific, targeted content and organizing it according to a content calendar, so that you are consistently building an audience, acclimating them to your brand, and making purchases!

Step 7: Put It to Use!

The final stage after creating your content calendar will be to put everything into action! This is discussed in chapter 8, where I demonstrate how to take explicit, consistent action on everything I have demonstrated in this book.

Chapter 3: Selecting Superior Affiliate Products

Affiliate marketing is a great way to make money online with minimal effort, and it works remarkably well, but it is not perfect. In other words, you may not achieve the immediate success you anticipate if you choose the wrong product or market it to the wrong audience. In this case, a significant portion of your performance will depend on selecting the appropriate product. Below is more information in depth. Most individuals, when deciding what to sell, proceed to their preferred affiliate network (ClickBank, JVZoo, or WSOPro) and browse the products with the highest commission rates and the most sales. Those numbers indicate that other people are earning a considerable amount of money, so it stands to reason that you will as well. It's as simple as "cut and paste" to replicate their accomplishment! However, if that is all you do, you are committing an error. The vast majority of the top-ranked results will cover generic topics such as "make money online," "date successfully," and "get in shape quickly." If you choose to advertise one of these publications, you will be competing with everyone else selling the exact same book or a book that is very similar to yours. After only a few days online, many internet users have grown weary of the constant ads for "work from home" opportunities. Additionally, these fields are among the most competitive online. It is nearly impossible to reach the top of Google's search results for "Make Money Online eBook" or "Build Muscle" if you do not have a fashionable website or mailing list. This action puts you in a position to fail.

Choose something that serves a subset of the population. You may discover an eBook that teaches flower arrangers how to monetize their craft, for instance. There are fewer opportunities for enthusiasm and exposure, but your offering is now truly unique. In addition, posting on a few floral blogs makes it simple to contact these flower arrangers. And it should be much easier to rank at the top of search engine results for "flower arranging eBook" with a link to your sales page. Additionally, it provides a unique selling factor that facilitates marketing. However, it is preferable to investigate the available distribution channels. Who do you know that could be useful? Where can a sizable population be reached? Why are they concerned with this? Before deciding on a product, you should evaluate your sales strategy and the most effective channels for reaching your target market. This is the success formula, and it can be utilized repeatedly. If your website is renowned and has a large audience, it makes sense that you would wish to sell to that demographic.

Also, remember that you can choose to sell many items. The simplicity with which new products can be added to or removed from a store's catalog is a significant advantage of selling digital products. There are both benefits and drawbacks to selling a variety of products. If you have a large website and employ persuasive persuasion techniques, selling multiple items simultaneously can be quite profitable. This also affords you the flexibility to set various prices for distinct customers. However, if you focus on a single product at a time, you will be able to generate more interest in that product and streamline your website so that consumers are directed directly to the checkout page. Buying Actual Products The selection process for tangible objects is somewhat distinct. Again, the objective is to select items of value for the content you've created and the average website visitor. In addition, they must be of high quality and satisfy an actual need.

There is no need to place a large bet on a purchase and pray for the best. You need not fret about stockpiling fidget spinners in a product-filled box. You may therefore go with the flow and test everything to determine what works. To appeal to the widest possible audience and generate the most revenue, you should still offer a variety of products at different price points. Therefore, getting the person to visit the website the link leads to is more crucial than making a sale of the item itself. Find a web hosting service and launch your website immediately. Create a new page, then copy and paste your sales copy and affiliate link onto it. Everything is in place for you to begin selling and make a profit. The next chapter will concentrate on this subsequent stage.

Chapter 4: Launching And Enhancing Your Website's Search Engine Visibility

It is extremely hazardous to optimize new websites with limited funds, but search engine optimization is essential for businesses. High-quality content and search engine optimization are the two pillars that keep your business afloat. Remember that people equal money, and that optimized content attracts relevant people to your business, who can easily be converted into customers.

If the content is not optimized correctly and precisely, your business will generate nil traffic. On-page SEO is advantageous for businesses of all sizes, but it is primarily recommended for small businesses because it accelerates growth.

You must optimize not only your content but also your keyboards, URLs, product descriptions, meta tags, and product links in order to dominate your market niche. To generate traffic to your website, you must optimize your website's content in these areas;

1- Make Certain Your URL Is Simple to Remember

The majority of content management system providers permit you to edit or modify URLs. As a case study, WordPress allows you to reformat your title and posts into a readable URL. Installing the Yoast SEO plug-in on your website is necessary to alter or edit any URL in your WordPress dashboard, as it enables users to read and comprehend your content with ease.

How To Enhance Your Site

1- Use pertinent keywords in your title and subheading

Always utilize keyboards with a high search volume and little or no competition. This increases your search engine optimization score and search engine visibility. To determine the appropriate keyboard to use, you must use a sophisticated keyword research tool because free ones do not provide detailed information, but with paid ones, you can obtain all the information you require, including the competition, search volume, and performance of each keyword.

2- Publish Trending Content Trending content, such as videos, images, parodies, and GIFs, encourages people to interact with your content.

3-Include pertinent tags in your heading.

Including pertinent tags in your heading helps to summarize your content in your audience's consciousness. This helps them determine whether or not your content is relevant to their interests. Your heading should be well-structured and well-written, as a poorly written heading will reduce your click-through rate.

This means that if your heading is unattractive or fails to make a good impression on your audience, it will have a negative effect on your business organically. Always attempt to use H1 for headings and H2-H6 for subheadings, as this enables the algorithm to comprehend your content.

Utilize fonts that are simple to read and ensure that your content is extremely informative, as most people scan text for the main idea before perusing it in its entirety.

How To Format Your Subheadings

1- The initial page should include pertinent keywords.

Mastering these marketing strategies provides you an advantage when studying SEO. I strongly suggest you use as many pertinent keywords as feasible in your first paragraph. Your first paragraph should contain the most crucial information about your content, as this is the paragraph that captures the reader's attention and encourages them to continue reading.

Any poorly written paragraph has produced a disconnect between the content and the audience.

2- Offer Hyperlinks To Previous Content

Including links to previous content aids in establishing a rapport with your audience. The algorithm enjoys it when users can easily navigate your website, and when they spend more time on your web page, it indicates that your content is extremely informative. This increases your website's organic visibility because Google prefers to display quality content on the first page.

In addition, effective web navigation increases visits, traffic, and site optimization. Use the PPC marketing strategy to analyze how people discover and navigate your websites for the best results.

3- Track Your Internet Speed

Visitors will not trust a website with a slow page load time. It is difficult to rank well if your website's speed is exceedingly slow, and for a better user experience, your website's speed should score between 85% and 90%.

What Are Your Strengths?

How you promote your affiliate offers will largely hinge on your strengths. Therefore, if you are a personable person who can speak for a considerable amount of time without stumbling (or if you want to be more personal and practice talking; you don't have to be perfect at first), you may want to consider doing video because it allows for a more intimate connection with people. People perceive your presence. They associate a visage with the name and subject you are discussing.

And people will likely trust you more than if you only have a blog post with no photo of yourself or mention of your name. People do business with those they know, like, and trust; therefore, video marketing is an effective method to promote your affiliate products.

I am not particularly good at public speaking or interpersonal skills. The majority of the time (even when I am) I speak with a monotone voice and don't appear particularly enthusiastic. RBF has afflicted me my entire existence. Even though I was overjoyed to see my wife walk down the aisle on our wedding day, I appeared angry. It also appears this way on video.

Due to this, I've recently taken to making TikTok videos because they have a shorter format, are easy to create, and if I make a mistake, I simply change the camera angle and repeat the next line again. If I appear angry in a footage, it doesn't take much effort to put on a huge smile and reshoot.

If you are more technically-inclined and enjoy writing but dislike long-form writing, social posts are the way to go. It may not always appear that social media users have a long attention span, but consider the popular posts. Many of them are short- to medium-length narrative posts that communicate with their audience.

And if you're a little shy and don't want to do video, but don't like writing either, you can always do audio, such as a podcast, to reach people and assist them. You can also do invisible videos on YouTube, which you can learn more about here: https://www.mastersalesfunnels.com/faceless-youtube-channel/.

Also, if you have a lot of money and are reading this book, you can always pay for advertisements that lead to your content, which then leads to your affiliate offers.

There are numerous rules within affiliate programs, typically prohibiting the use of keywords related to the branded terms for affiliate offers in advertisements. There are laws against running ads directly to affiliate offers; therefore, you must have content (a blog, video, or podcast) that leads to your sales page (a bridge page), and from there to the affiliate offer.

How you will promote your affiliate offers and drive traffic to your Bridge Page Funnel is entirely dependent on the resources you have at your disposal and your individual skills. More on these funnel types to come.

Chapter 5: Publish Your Post

"The Content Is King" therefore, are you contemplating writing your first blog post?

So let me assist you to compose your first article on your blog. First of all, I'd like to congratulate you on setting up your WordPress blog successfully; now it's time to write some posts for your new site.

In order to generate a blog post, you must: Dashboard Post Insert

Now, I'll provide you with some tips that will enable you to compose your first outstanding article.

Utilize appropriate titles, header, and subtitles

Use powerful phrases such as "Top 10" and "Best" in your title.

Always attempt to create a catchy title for your blog post.

Use I and You to strengthen your connection with your audience.

Avoid over-optimizing your post.

Utilize compressed images (use compresspng.com to compress images) (use compresspng.com to compress images).

Focus on the substance of the content and avoid copying and pasting from other sites.

Create content that is shareable

Optimize the article's duration

Use interlinking

Utilize the on-page SEO recommendations provided by your SEO plugin, such as Rank Maths, etc.

Do not utilize images from Google

Utilize royalty-free images from websites such as Pixabay, Pexels, etc.

I hope these guidelines make it easy for you to write your first blog post.

Your website must contain essential pages such as the About Us, Contact Us, Disclaimer, and Privacy policies pages.

To produce pages To add a new page, navigate to Dashboard > Pages > Add New.

About Us Page - You must include a description of yourself and your blog.

Contact Us Page - Using the contactform7 plugin, you can quickly create a contact page.

Disclaimer Page - You can search online for "Disclaimer Page Generator" to find free tools that will allow you to create your disclaimer page.

Privacy Policy Page - You can search the internet for "Privacy Policy Page Generator" to find free tools that will help you design your Privacy Policy page.

Always keep in mind that, when writing a post, you must adhere to the procedures recommended by your SEO plugin, such as RankMath, Yoast, etc...

Once your blog contains excellent content, the next step is to promote it.

Let's examine how to promote...

Affiliate Marketing

Making money while you slumber must be one of the best ways to supplement your income, right? Indeed, it's true. And the image you created in your mind is indeed POSSIBLE. How?

Affiliate Marketing is the answer to this inquiry.

Consequently, what is affiliate marketing?

Affiliate marketing is the practice of promoting other people's goods and services in exchange for a commission on each sale generated through your efforts. This is the simplest way to convey the term, and it sounds familiar because it refers to the traditional method of commission-based compensation. Now, allow me to expand on this term.

Affiliate marketing is a form of advertising that enables businesses and organizations to compensate third-party individuals for generating sales on their website. The third-party individual or organization will utilize its influence to persuade consumers to purchase the respective organization's product or service. Affiliates are third-party individuals or businesses who are compensated for generating sales for an organization's products or services.

You have likely encountered "sponsored posts" on multiple websites. This constitutes affiliate marketing. The organization releases the commission to the affiliate only if the consumer clicks to purchase the advertised product or service. Therefore, affiliate marketing is a stride forward in the generation of passive income for affiliates based on commissions. Bloggers, for instance, have an audience and can use their influence to persuade their followers to purchase products from a particular website. If the consumer purchases the product or service from the website in question, the website must pay the blogger a commission.

The quantity of the commission is predetermined by both parties. Affiliate marketing is a four-component performance-based marketing strategy.

The vendor of the product or service is the merchant. Therefore, the merchant is the website that wishes to advertise its product or service. Other terms for merchant include distributor, retailer, brand, and vendor.

An affiliate is a person or business that promotes the seller's product or service. They receive a commission for their promotion efforts, which is paid out following the sale. Affiliates use advertisements, links, and banners to promote the product or service of the respective company. Publisher is another prevalent term used to refer to the affiliate.

A consumer is a purchaser of the affiliate-promoted and merchant-offered product or service.

The network is the digital platform where the strategy is executed (website, social media networking sites, online newsletters, or blogs). Multiple affiliate networks have been developed to seamlessly manage payments and product deliveries.

Affiliate marketing has become one of the most popular ways for consumers to earn money online. Affiliates and merchants have access to an ocean of opportunities when they have a comprehensive comprehension of the format. Even consumers can obtain the finest bargains in the bargaining process. Therefore, the marketing strategy may be advantageous for all users.

Chapter 6: How Do You Get Individuals To Speak?

Create a unique screen name that piques people's curiosity about who you are and what you do, so that they will contact you. The chosen name will establish the tone for all future conversations. Assume that your screen name is Life Style Designer and that you run a website that facilitates dynamic personal lifestyle changes to enhance your life. You may write to other life coaches and say that you appreciate your job and wonder if they do as well. If they dislike what you're doing, they will let you know. Now is your opportunity to explain what you do.

Typically, you will be the one asking inquiries. This is the key to prequalifying individuals. Ask queries, and you will be able to determine after a few brief conversations whether the individual has the potential to join your organization. You will recognize them by their responses to your questions.

When speaking with someone online via instant messenger, avoid sending lengthy updates about your activities. They are uninterested and do not wish to hear it. Proceed with caution and distribute information based on their responses to your notes. Go slowly, employ your intellect, be concise, and read between the lines. You WILL be able to determine when they have lost or are losing interest based on their responses.

Community Collaboration

Community networking entails promoting your business/product/service in a community context in online communities such as Ryze, Yahoo, Direct Match, My Space, Circle of Friends, and other forums populated by like-minded people and marketers. Community networking can be incorporated into any online business. Simply put, your purpose is to inform people about what you have to offer.

You can locate people by conducting searches and contacting them based on the information contained in their profiles. Finding people's email addresses can be a bit of a challenge, but with a little Googling and Internet cross-checking, you can find the email addresses of the people you wish to contact. If you know that they are already Internet marketers (or that they are not), adjust your approach accordingly.

Community networking can result in company expansion, sales, general marketing, recruitment, job searching, information sharing, strategic alliances, and joint ventures, among other benefits. Business expansion and community networking are inextricably linked.

Relationships are key to community networking. You are attempting a convergence or a meeting of the minds. If the answer is yes, you collaborate to make the connection a reality. It is typically simpler and less intimidating to discuss collaboration as opposed to acquisition.

Creating connections is an end in and of itself, not solely a means to an end. Despite the interpersonal aspects of your approach to the prospect, your ultimate goal is still to make a sale.

The conventional view of the sales relationship with prospects is that a salesperson's performance is measured in terms of sales, not relationships. This is the problem with the majority of traditional online marketing strategies. The connection element is absent. People disregard marketing communications from strangers with whom they have no connection. If, however, you have a relationship with them, they will likely always open your emails. Therefore, you must focus on the connection itself and not just the short-term goal of making a sale.

What other steps can you take to build relationships while engaging in community networking? Conduct market research, and listen more than you speak. Typically, marketing organizations are quite forthright with their opinions on various topics. You require this information immediately.

Considered an expert in your field will increase your social stature and give you greater access to your audience. Speak out in a forum, blog, or mailing list to reach countless individuals. Discuss what you know best; if you make it creative or thought-provoking, you will be cited and linked. That is incredible exposure! In addition, while you're at it, include a link to your company's website or blog in the signature of every email you send, every Web transaction you complete, and every profile you create. Invaluable exposure.

Via social networks, word-of-mouth spreads rapidly. Utilize this fact while engaging in community networking, and you will soon have people from all over the world seeking out what you have to offer.

ROI - Return On Investment

If you are investing money in affiliate marketing activities, you must be aware of your return on investment. Before calculating your net profit (commissions), you must account for all campaign-related expenses. This will immediately inform you of your efforts' profitability. You want to achieve the highest possible ROI.

Ad Blockers

Ad blockers are pieces of software that users install in their browsers to prevent advertisements from displaying. It is estimated that 15% of Internet users presently employ ad blockers, a number that has increased significantly over time.

Ad blockers are a negative for affiliate marketers. If your advertisement does not appear, you will not receive commissions. Unfortunately, dishonest marketers have contributed significantly to the development of this technology. There is nothing you can do to stop ad blocking at this time.

SEO is Search Engine Optimization.

The greatest visitor traffic for your affiliate offers is targeted traffic. This indicates that the visitor is interested in your niche or a particular product you offer. If you can achieve a high ranking for your content on major search engines such as Google and YouTube (for videos), you may attract a large number of free visitors to your offerings.

Optimize your content to increase your odds of ranking highly in search engines. You must conduct keyword research and ensure that your title, meta description, and content contain the most pertinent terms. SEO is a highly complex topic, and there are numerous online training courses available.

Separate Testing

Often referred to as A/B testing, split testing contrasts the performance of two or more advertisements for the same affiliate offer. Using sponsored traffic solutions from Google, YouTube, and other major sources, split testing is possible. Utilize the provided data to determine which advertisement is performing the best.

Tracking Links A tracking link will inform you of the origin of your visitors. You may employ a variety of traffic sources for your affiliate marketing campaigns, and you must determine which ones are generating the best results. For this purpose, some affiliate networks will provide you with tracking connections.

Dual-Level Affiliate Programs

In a two-tier affiliate program, in addition to receiving a commission for any sales you generate, you also receive a portion of the commissions generated by the affiliates you recruited. The more affiliates you recruit, the greater your likelihood of generating additional revenue.

Flexibility and liberty are inherent.

Affiliate marketing offers a high degree of freedom, independence, and adaptability, regardless of whether it is your primary or secondary source of income. Affiliate marketing, in contrast to most regular employment, allows you to make some decisions on your own, such as determining your schedule and working hours. Similarly, when you have free time, you have the option to choose your partners or employers. You can maximize and maximize your productivity by selecting a comfortable environment and schedule.

Affiliate marketing does not have to be your only source of income; it can be a secondary revenue stream. In reality, you may need supplemental income even if you have a job and have no plans to resign. Affiliate marketing should be considered your finest alternative. Since you already have a stable income, you can use it to earn more money without feeling imminent pressure to succeed. Consequently, you can approach your undertaking with a great deal more lightheartedness and take your time determining the best approach and strategy. It could be your primary source of income, and it can help you get paid faster than looking for employment if you choose to do so.

The benefits of affiliate marketing are not exhaustive. Obviously, the benefits associated with the market's scale could be just as substantial. There may be risks involved, but the benefits may ultimately outweigh them.

Chapter 7: Developing Professionalism

Although there are no formal education requirements to become an affiliate marketer, formal education can equip you with the skills and knowledge necessary for success in this field. Consider enrolling in a degree program or certification course in order to acquire essential industry knowledge and relevant marketing skills. Degree and certification programs may be offered online or in your community. Marketing, communications, and business development may be beneficial in this field.

The eMarketing Institute offers a certification that is extensively utilized by affiliate marketers. This educational institution provides a free online certification course for aspiring affiliate marketers who want to learn from seasoned professionals and hone the skills required to succeed in this industry.

The commercial aspect of affiliate marketing

A business compensates a creative for access to its existing clientele through an affiliate network. Typically, these affiliates consist of bloggers, social media influencers, websites, digital platforms, and other digital pioneers.

Developing an audience for your brand requires time and effort. Some marketers believe that it makes more sense to collaborate with producers whose fan base closely resembles their intended audience.

This strategy benefits businesses and affiliate marketers alike. By utilizing their affiliates' built-in network, businesses can avoid the time and effort required to find the ideal consumer. Businesses can be certain that they are only paying for qualified leads because affiliate marketers are only compensated based on sales volume.

It is a straightforward method for affiliate marketers to generate revenue from their platforms. Numerous affiliate marketers have amassed substantial audiences on their blogs, social networking sites, and other private channels. Affiliate marketing facilitates marketers' sponsorship of products and passive income generation.

There are numerous options available to businesses for locating and collaborating with affiliates to develop brand connections. Your strategy for developing an affiliate marketing program may vary based on your company's brand, product, and industry, but there are a few fundamental steps that every business should take first.

Taxes payable by the affiliate marketer

Affiliate marketers are taxed in the United States just like any other occupation. If your income is less than $600, you only qualify for this exemption. Once you reach this threshold, you are required to file taxes with the IRS, specifically Schedule C, during tax season. To report loss or gain, single-member LLCs and sole proprietors must complete Schedule C, a tax form. Examples include small business owners, freelancers, and persons with a second job. If you still have concerns about Schedule C, you can consult your accountant.

Administrator, Subsidiary

Some subsidiary organizations have specialized offshoot administrators available to assist you in achieving success. They can communicate with you directly via email or courier service. It is prudent to maintain contact with your partner director, as they are typically aware of the most advantageous subsidiary conversion offers.

Subsidiary Establishment

A member network is a website that grants access to numerous subsidiary offers. Clickbank.com, one of the most well-known member networks, grants access to a large number of diverse subsidiary offers.

Most affiliate organizations will provide you with detailed information regarding their affiliate offers. You can ordinarily determine the notoriety of a product or administration, its conversion rate, and the commission you can earn, among other things. Associate organizations bring together product and service merchants and collaborators. Unless a vendor has a partner program, they will utilize a member organization to promote their offerings to subsidiaries. Some affiliate organizations use automated endorsements to promote their products and services. Others will expect you to obtain approval from specific item vendors.

Offshoot Supply

A partner offer is a single product or service that you can promote in exchange for a commission. Most partner organizations will list the subsidiary offers they have available and provide important metrics, such as sales volume, conversion rates, and so forth.

For each subsidiary offering, you will typically have access to a distinct member interface. When one of your visitors clicks on this connection, they will be redirected to the product or administration's sales page, and you will be credited. If they make purchases, you'll earn commissions.

Associate Program

A subsidiary program is a framework that enables product and service retailers to enroll and pay commissions to subsidiaries. The merchant can determine the commission rate for each transaction. Partners will use the program to register as a subsidiary and obtain their exceptional subsidiary connections.

Standard Request Cost

This is where the offshoot organization will reveal the average request value for every associate proposal. Numerous items and services have revisions where the customer can enhance their purchase. These are referred to as "back end" offers and will be presented to the consumer after they have purchased the "front end" product or service.

The average request value will evaluate these redesign offers. You will see the average amount of money that customers expend when purchasing a particular product. This is significant because you will typically earn commissions on both revisions and front-end sales.

Rewards

Associate marketing can be extremely serious, and if you can offer related benefits to customers that other affiliates cannot, you will experience a benefit. In the make money on the web or Internet marketing niche, you will see a great deal of rewards offered.

Assuming you will advance a member offer that demonstrates how to create an email summary and offer, you could provide your email swipes as a bonus. These are messages with high conversion rates that you have utilized in the past. If a customer believes you offer the finest rewards, they will use your member link to make a purchase, earning you a commission.

Rates to Navigate (NR)

The active visitor clicking percentage (NR) is an important metric that measures the number of times your associate proposal interface is selected. As a rate, it is determined by the number of impressions your connection receives. If you can achieve a high NR, you will have a greater chance of earning more commissions.

Suppose you have a list of 10,000 supporters' email addresses. You send an email containing your member link, and 5,000 of your subscribers open it. This means your connection has received 5,000 impressions. Your CTR is

10% if 500 of your supporters click on your connection.

Rate of Transformation

Another essential measurement. Using our model for calculating conversion rates, you send 500 people to the offshoot offer you are promoting. The number of people who make a purchase is used to calculate your exchange rate.

Therefore, if 50 individuals out of 500 make a purchase, your conversion rate is 10%. Similar to conversion rates, the greater your navigation rates, the better. Partners can evaluate exchange rates for different offers. They can use paid traffic to determine how many of their clicks result in sales. If the conversion rate is high, they can invest in more traffic to increase their cash flow.

Treats

A treat is a small piece of code that identifies a visitor who touched on one of your partner's joins. The partner program or system will typically remember treats for a predetermined amount of time.

Consider that the proposed transaction has a 30-day treatment period. This means that if the visitor returns to the deals page for the product or service within this timeframe, the first partner who referred them will be credited with the sale and receive the commission.

CPA - Cost Per Activity

Cost per action (CPA) advertising is where subsidiaries will receive a commission if a visitor to their member site completes a specific action. This may involve inputting their email address, completing a simple form, providing their postal code, etc.

Numerous member advertisers favor CPA offers because no transaction is required to earn a commission. Since the visitor is not required to make a purchase, the conversion rates for CPA offers are typically much higher. However, commission rates for CPA offers are frequently lower than those for deal making.

CPL (Cost Per Lead)

Cost-per-lead (CPL) advertising typically requires a visitor to provide their email address, call a specific phone number, or provide another contact method. CPL offers do not require a transaction to occur for an affiliate advertiser to receive a commission.

CPS (Cost Per Sale)

Cost per Sale (CPS) is the most well-known subsidiary proposition variety. Each time a visitor referred by the affiliate makes a purchase, a predetermined commission is paid to the affiliate. CPS offers typically offer higher commission rates than CPA and CPL offers. However, this is not typically the case, so be careful to complete your work.

Actuality Feeds

Some offshoot organizations or endeavors will provide their subsidiaries with an information feed for use on their website. A document contains the products and services that a promoter sells, including the following: • Product or service names • Prices for the products or services • Images for the products or services • Descriptions

• Novel member joins

A partner can utilize this data input to display the entire product catalog on their website. If the visitor clicks on the affiliate link in the information feed to learn more and then makes a purchase, the affiliate will receive a commission.

Profit Per Click (PPC) is another important metric you should be aware of. All partner organizations or programs may provide CPC figures for their products and services. A PPC is conveyed in monetary terms, such as $10, and represents a proportion of the commission amount that any subsidiary will earn for each click of their partner connection.

Impressions

Impressions are the instances in which your advertisement or associate connection is displayed. A few websites charge publicists on the basis of "cost per thousand impressions (CPM)." With email advertising, impressions are the number of times a subscriber opens your email and views your partner's interface.

Location of arrival

A presentation page is a website page to which you direct visitors who click on your connections. This could be an instantaneous link to the product's or administration's business page, for example. Currently, astute partner advertisers are directing their visitors to their points of arrival as opposed to a deals page.

Obtaining the guest's email address is likely the most compelling reason for doing this. Once you have their email address, you can send them directly to the vendor deals page. You can also use an entry page or a landing page to warm up your visitor before they see the merchant deals page.

Some advertising organizations prohibit sending visitors directly to an offers page. Google and Facebook will require that you arrive at an educational destination. Where you send the guest thereafter is up to you.

Leads If you wish to achieve success as a member advertiser, you must pursue both leads and transactions. By using a presentation page to collect the email address of your guest, you generate a valuable lead with whom you can communicate in the future. A portion of the prospects will make purchases through your affiliate link, resulting in additional commissions.

Email prospects are significant because you can communicate with your visitors at any time. If you merely send a visitor to the merchant's deals page, you may lose them forever if they do not make a purchase. Not everyone will purchase the first time they see an advertisement. Collecting email leads enables you to communicate directly with your visitors again.

Chapter 8: How To Select Affiliate Products Intelligently

Remember that you also have the option to sell objects. You can quickly add or remove products from your website without spending days writing or formatting! There are advantages and disadvantages to retailing multiple products. Selling multiple products is advantageous if you have a large website and use softsale techniques (refer to the following chapter). This also enables you to offer a range of prices to various customer types. However, focusing on a single product at a time will enable you to generate more buzz and excitement around that product, as well as create a more streamlined website that directs customers to a single page: the purchase page.

Selecting Physical Goods

Picking up genuine objects is an unusual interaction. Again, the procedure should be to select items that are relevant to your content and to the average website visitor. Concurrently, they should and that fulfills a genuine need.

Fortunately, there is no compelling reason to make a bold prediction and confront a challenge by purchasing large quantities of items. You will not be leaving at twirly concerts! That means that if you have a stockroom full of items, you can pursue various avenues and throw everything against the wall to see what adheres. I do recommend, however, that you offer a variety of products with varying price tags in order to cater to every type of customer.BUT also keep in mind that you earn a commission on all purchases made after the customer visits Amazon.

This implies that the primary objective should be to get the user to click the link and visit the page, perhaps even more so than marketing the product itself! Obtain a web host and create your website. Create a new web page and place the duplicate sales page along with your affiliate link on it. You are currently prepared to begin selling and generating revenue! We'll examine this subsequent stage in the section that follows.

Be daring. Be distinct. Be ardent. Then, select a product that addresses the same audience. Have no time for that? Not to fret about the items below.

Inserting Your Link

There are additional alternatives As an affiliate marketer, selling is incredibly simple. You are given one link to promote a product, from which you can generate sales and revenue regardless of where you position it. The dilemma then becomes: where do you place it? The vast majority of us will position our link on a landing page or sales page, but this is just one option. In this section, we will examine how that functions, as well as a number of additional options.

Developing a Selling Page

A sales page is a web page designed specifically for the purpose of selling a product or service. This means that it will not provide any additional content (no articles) or links or advertisements. You do not want anything that could potentially detract from the product you are selling.

The design of a sales page is typically very long and narrow, which encourages readers to continue scrolling and, consequently, devote more time in the process of reading your content. This makes it much more difficult for them to depart without making a purchase, as they will feel they have wasted their time! However, the most essential aspect is the writing. Correctly crafting your sales pitch will allow you to convert this captive audience into eager customers. Persuasive writing is an extremely potent instrument that can transform you into a Jedi master of marketing. These are not the droids that you seek... Ultimately, if you know how to use words to persuade an audience, you will be much more effective at making sales, getting people to subscribe to your list, and attaining any other objective you're pursuing. How then does one acquire this superpower? Here are some helpful hints...

Withdraw consideration:

People are in a hurry and would prefer not to read extensive amounts of text. If you have any intention of persuading your audience, you must first motivate them to read what you have to say. How would you proceed? One strategy is to begin with a bold assertion. Using a narrative structure is another technique for capturing the audience's attention. We typically find it very difficult to distance ourselves from a story without becoming completely detached!

Appeal to statistical data points: People are typically not inclined to trust you; after all, they've never met you and they know you have something to offer them. Rather, let the numbers represent you at that juncture. The more statistics you can cite and the more experts you can cite, the more compelling your argument will become.

- Expect:

Try to anticipate the concerns that your readers will have and then promptly address them. For instance, you can mention that there are a plethora of enticing-sounding online offers, but emphasize that this is not "just another scam."

- Moderate gamble:

People are ordinarily susceptible to "misfortune revulsion." This indicates that they are quicker to hold onto what they already possess than to acquire something new. You want to eliminate any element of chance at that time by providing unconditional guarantees and complimentary preliminary work.

Above all:

recognize the incentive. This is the close-to-home estimation of your item: how you guarantee it will alter the lives of your readers. For instance, if you are selling a wellness eBook, you should be aware that you are not truly selling a wellness eBook! What you're really peddling is the sensation of having boundless energy, ripped abs, and abundant confidence. You should really hone in on that! Address the heart and endeavor to evoke emotion in the reader, preferably the desire to purchase your product.

Keep in mind:

Numerous electronic items will have immediate deals pages similar to this, meaning you can simply copy the content discount to use on your own page. With your offers page, you now only need to direct your audience to that page to begin generating conversions. This should be possible via communications and by advancing your web-based entertainment item. You could recollect advertisements for the product for your website's sidebar and elsewhere.

Creating a Store

If you are selling various member items (which is also a generally excellent practice), you can create a store from which to sell them. This means that you will feature and promote products that are relevant to your brand, as you would in an online business store. The only real difference is that when a customer clicks on your product, they will now be taken to an external page.This is simple to accomplish; for example, you can use the WooCommerce web-based business module for WordPress. This will allow you to create a store on your website where people can view items. It supports ancillary content, so that if someone clicks on an item, they will be redirected to a new page using your external reference.

More Sales Channels

However, what about embedding seams within the content of your articles? This is a feature that few users take advantage of, but it is an excellent method for customizing a website or blog. Simply elaborate on any aspect of the subject you're interested in discussing and then insert a secondary connection. Thus, you can promote the item without pretense, and anyone who is interested in your content can select it. It's similar to adding AdSense to your page, except you earn a higher commission and have the ability to effectively encourage people to click the link. You may speak the truth about how it generates income for you! In many regions of the world, the law requires you to deny that you are profiting from the sale of these items. You can accomplish this by using a module that adds a message to the bottom of each page on your website; however, remember! The top ten list is one of the best types of content for selling affiliate products. If you're in the health and fitness industry, you can create a launch article highlighting the best home gym equipment, and if you're in the technology industry, you can create a launch article highlighting the best PCs on the market. Whatever you choose to do, this is ideal for generating clicks and revenue, and it lends itself well to complex scraps, which can help your content rank higher in the SERPs (Search Engine Results Pages). In addition, nothing prevents you from including a within the body of a partner connect email. This is an excellent method for contacting people directly within their inbox when they may be receptive to your offers. In eBooks, offshoot links are also permitted. If you are selling a digital product or providing one for free, you can include hyperlinks in your PDF. People reading this will likely be captivated by your image and consequently more likely to purchase what you recommend. These are qualified leads, making this the ideal place to endeavor to sell significantly more expensive items. Imagine selling a computerized product for $20 each, and then receiving additional funds from each person who reads the book and follows your advice. Or, what about incorporating a member interface onto an actual flier or flyer? Utilizing a more significant and basic URL and redirecting it to your subsidiary connection is the most effective method to utilize this feature. Thus, you can effectively advertise your product face-to-face! The main point of these concepts is to demonstrate that you don't necessarily need to be actively selling the product: you can attempt a soft sell by simply adding a connection, perhaps with an image.

This works exceptionally well for actual products (especially if you use a well-designed icon and the item is effectively connected to the page's content). If you have a popular website with a large number of viewers and a great deal of content, simply interspersing affiliate links throughout can result in a flood of sales... and they all add up! There are many more methods to utilize offshoot joins; you just need to be creative. You may be surprised by what works best for you and your product after conducting research and experimenting with a variety of methods.

Commercial keywords

Commercial keywords are search queries in which the user expresses an interest in a product or service.

These terms can be as straightforward as a brand or product-specific search. For instance, a search for "Nike shoes" Alternatively, they may include additional terms such as "Review," "best," or "top."

Because people who conduct these queries are typically in the market for a product or service, these keywords can be an effective means of reaching your target audience.

Depending on where the individual is in the purchase decision process, they may be ready to make a purchase immediately or require additional information. For instance, a person may be aware that they require a specific form of product, but they wish to evaluate various alternatives prior to making a final decision.

Reviews, comparisons, and how-to articles are therefore excellent for targeting commercial search phrases.

Transactional search terms

Transactional keywords are queries in which the user intends to make a purchase. These are the most valuable keywords because they are used by individuals who are most likely to make a purchase.

Typical transactional terms include "buy", "discount", and "for sale".

In most cases, the searcher already has the necessary information and will likely make a purchase after tapping on one of Google's results.

Pro-Tip

A decent affiliate marketing course will teach you the ins and outs of generating traffic for affiliate marketing purposes. Here is a list of the top online affiliate marketing courses.

Promote items that people are actively seeking to purchase

After narrowing in on excellent keyword targets, you should select the products you wish to promote.

In the next few stages of this guide on how to make money as an affiliate marketer, we will discuss a number of important characteristics to seek out.

The primary objective is to promote affiliate products with steady demand.

The idea behind this is straightforward. If you want your marketing efforts to result in sales, you must promote products that people are actively seeking.

When developing a plan to attract targeted traffic, you will naturally gain an understanding of the varieties of products people are seeking. Additionally, you will be exposed to specific solutions and brands so that you are familiar with the best options in your niche.

Keep a watch on the level of competition in the niche while searching for products with a strong interest. The more competitive the keywords are for specific product varieties, the more difficult it will be to rank and drive traffic to your website.

The optimal equilibrium consists of products with high demand and manageable levels of competition.

Using Google Trends is one method to understand the demand for a particular niche. With the platform, you can track the evolution of interest in specific keywords and topics.

Thus, you can ensure that the products you're considering have enduring appeal and are not just a passing fad.

4. Promote Selling Products

In addition to marketing products that are actively searched for, it is essential to market products that sell. This refers to advocating products with a high rate of conversion.

Conversion rate is a metric that measures the proportion of individuals who purchase your products after viewing them.

A high conversion rate indicates that you are maximizing the value of your website traffic.

Start your search for high-converting products by identifying the best market solutions. Naturally, high-quality products from reputable labels will perform better than inferior products.

Price is an additional factor that you must take into account. In general, cheaper products convert at a higher rate than their more expensive counterparts.

The essence of a product will also impact its conversion rate. If you market commodities, you can anticipate greater conversion rates. Conversely, you may experience lower conversions if you promote high-consideration products that consumers want to carefully evaluate before making a decision.

Promote only those products with high affiliate commissions.

Affiliate marketing will help you make money if you promote products with a high rate of conversion, but it is also essential to promote products with high commission rates.

If you earn higher commissions per order, you will require fewer transactions to reach your income objectives.

High-Ticket Affiliate Program Examples;

To place this into context, let's examine a few different scenarios.

In the first instance, you advertise common consumer goods priced between $10 and $20 from Amazon. The affiliate program pays a 5% commission on each transaction, so you will receive between $0.50 and $1 per sale.

If 10% of your traffic converts, it would take 10 visitors to generate $1 and 1,000 visitors to generate $100.

Compare this to an affiliate program in which you promote a $100 product and earn 50% of the transaction price, or $50, per sale.

This offer requires only two transactions to generate $100. This indicates that you could monetize 1% of your traffic and earn $100 with only 200 visitors.

Product price, commission rates, and recurring payments are the three most important factors that will determine your affiliate commissions.

Sales price

In nearly every affiliate program, the selling price of the product will determine how much you earn per sale. This is because the majority of programs pay a commission on each sale. Others pay a fixed fee that reflects the item's price and the customer's potential lifetime value.

For instance, the Shopify affiliate program will pay you twice the first monthly fee of a subscriber.

Commission Expense

The commission rate is the proportion of the product's price that you earn per transaction. It can have a significant impact on your affiliate marketing earnings.

Two distinct affiliate programs may both offer $100 products, but if one offers a 50% commission and the other a 10% commission, one is significantly more lucrative than the other.

Repeated reimbursements

Some of the most effective high-ticket affiliate programs pay commissions on recurrent revenue. These are typically subscription-based products, such as web hosting plans and other software services.

Affiliate products with recurring commissions can be among the most lucrative because you can maximize the value of each customer.

Chapter 9: Optimize Your Affiliate Links In Order To Gain More Clicks

Affiliate links allow you to profit from transactions. When a customer purchases an affiliate product after selecting your link, the affiliate merchant will credit you with the sale and pay you the agreed-upon commission amount.

Therefore, the finest products will be of little use if no one clicks on your affiliate links. In order to maximize the number of individuals who click on your links, it is necessary to optimize their placement.

However, this does not imply that you should scatter links throughout your content. You should only include links when they are relevant and avoid including them when they do not suit your content.

The addition of an excessive number of links can negatively affect the user experience and result in missed sales.

As a general rule, you should position your links near the beginning of your content. Many readers will not reach the end of your posts, and others will likely gloss over the details along the way. By placing your links at the outset of your content, you increase the likelihood that they will be viewed by more people.

Here are some additional optimization recommendations for your affiliate links.

Chapter 10: The Positives Of Drop Shipping

First, drop shipping allows you to test and sell new products quickly without having to purchase them in bulk.

This is intended for those unfamiliar with the concept of volume purchasing: Buying in bulk entails obtaining a large quantity of identical items all at once, as opposed to purchasing a single item via Drop shipping.

This means you will need to locate a place to store your belongings. Do not misunderstand; each has its benefits! Problematically, if you don't know if you can sell the product or if your target audience would like the product, you could wind up with a large quantity of items that you cannot sell.

The advantage of drop shipping is that you do not have to purchase hundreds or thousands of identical products before selling them on your website.

You can practically purchase them individually. This means that you only pay for products when they are purchased from your online store. Isn't that beautiful?

Yes, this has its own disadvantage, but the good news is that you can now determine if you can sell the product before making a large volume purchase.

If the product does not sell, you can swiftly move on to other things without worrying about remaining inventory in your warehouse, home, or other storage location.

Drop shipping can be lucrative, but only if you know when to stop. If your product is performing well and you have identified a market for it, purchasing it in bulk is a fantastic idea.

Initial expenses are quite low compared to those of retail outlets.

This one goes hand-in-hand with the previous one, as you do not need to purchase items in quantity to begin selling them in your online store.

Due to the fact that you do not need to keep inventory on hand, establishing a Drop shipping business is incredibly inexpensive. This also saves you money on warehouse fees and other expenses.

However, bear in mind that this is still a legitimate business and not a get-rich-quick scheme!

A Drop shipping store or an eCommerce store does not require you to pay rent, but you do need a mechanism to launch your business, such as Shopify, whose lowest plan costs $29 per month.

That is a substantial difference between retail establishment rent, correct?

You are not responsible for manufacturing, storing, or shipping the products.

Drop shipping is advantageous because your Drop shipping provider handles everything for you. They manage the shipping, storage, and production of the product.

This means that you are only responsible for marketing the product, while your Drop shipping provider handles the rest. Isn't that incredible?

Obviously, there is a downside to this; since you cannot see the products, there may be quality concerns.

This also means you can add additional items without fretting about storage space.

Acquire useful abilities

As previously stated, drop shipping is merely a fulfillment method.

The remaining aspects of eCommerce are unaltered. You will continue to learn skills such as internet-based marketing.

Copywriting

Conversion rate augmentation

Social media management

Obviously, there is much more!

Even if you decide to close your drop shipping business, you could utilize these skills.

You can establish a Drop Shipping store quickly.

Because it is so easy to create a Drop shipping store and begin selling the same day, many people are beginning to use Drop shipping.

Why is it so straightforward?

For instance, if you compare it to establishing a traditional "offline" retail store, you will see that there is an initial investment required.

You only pay for items when a customer places an order through your online business.

Not only is the financial investment distinct, but so too are the risks involved. Nothing has changed for the time being.

You can essentially create a Shopify store in a matter of minutes, and everything will be live within hours!

To separate out from the crowd of other Drop shippers who open their stores in a matter of hours, it is advisable to take your time when constructing your Drop shipping store.

Highly adaptable

If you so desire, you can sell to the entire globe.

Do you comprehend why?

Your Drop shipping provider can ship to any country in the world, so you have nothing to worry about when it comes to advertising in a new nation! There is still a remote chance that your supplier does not ship to that location.

In addition, you can discover Drop shipping suppliers in each country, including the United States. This will have its own benefits, including quicker shipping periods.

Because delivery from China can take between two and four weeks!

The ability to turn your store into a brand is an additional benefit of drop shipping that complements its extreme scalability.

You can also get started immediately with a branded Drop shipping store.

Chapter 11: How To Develop An Entrepreneurial Mindset

Things might occasionally go awry. If you make an error, one of your decisions could be defective. During such moments, you may feel defeated, injured, shattered, and despondent. You must however not give up. Instead, consider your error. Determine what went wrong and what you could have done to remedy the situation. Then attempt one more time.

Examine and verify any information that does not appear to be consistent if things don't make sense. Alternately, you may post your query in the social network group of your choosing. There are numerous Shopify instructional videos on YouTube. You may receive all the aid you require.

Whenever feasible, work with a dropshipping lifestyle coach.This is one of the best ways to ensure that you are never alone while traveling. In addition, the coach will assist you in avoiding some of the most common obstacles encountered by newcomers.

Keep in mind that you will be required to work extremely hard at first until your company acquires a reputation and a sizable customer base. Never give up; instead, whenever you feel like giving up, persist and seek assistance.

Even if your business is in its infancy, you can sell from multiple locations, list it on marketplaces, and generate thousands of dollars in monthly sales.

However, you may have to wait a while if you simply wait for people to visit your website. Traditional merchants may appear to be more profitable, but their expenses and overheads are substantially higher. As a result, you will fare much better as a dropshipper.

Frequent Dropshipping Errors 1. Being overly concerned with shipping costs

This may be concerning due to the substantial regional differences in transportation costs. However, you should not fret excessively about this. Decide what your priorities are in this regard, and then make your selection. To alleviate this tension, it is easier to establish a fixed rate of delivery.

2. Making it difficult to get order details

Customers will learn from the information on your website that placing an order is simple, stress-free, and fast. Customers often require evidence. To keep your clients informed, you must ensure that your suppliers keep you apprised of the order's status and provide approximate shipment dates.

3. limited brand recognition

Frequently, you will fail to highlight your brand so that buyers will see it again when they peruse. Include your brand's name and logo on as many pages as possible to continually and frequently remind customers of your brand.

Making a mess of customer purchases

This is another typical occurrence. Customers frequently click on the wrong object or purchase the wrong item. They occasionally place an order but then change their minds. Please notify your dropshipping provider if an order is canceled so that they can rescind it; otherwise, you risk receiving a poor rating.

5. Refund-related concerns

Returns occur frequently, and if they are not managed properly, they are typically chaotic. You should implement a complex return management system. You can avoid the anxiety associated with refunds in this way.

PPC Advertising and Other Forms of Advertising

However, what occurs if there are no listeners? What happens if you lack the readers' respect as a thought leader?

In this situation, you will need to determine how to attract visitors to your sales page. The good news is that Pay-Per-Click (PPC) platforms such as Facebook and AdWords make this straightforward.

PPC refers to an advertising model in which you only pay when someone acts on your ad. You determine the upper and lower limits of your budget, as well as your utmost "per click" expenditure. If you set your cost per click too low, your ad will not appear if there are a large number of competing ads in the same market.

You can target the audience for your Facebook advertising based on the information that social media users share. These include: • age • gender • location • interests and pastimes • position • income level • the interests of others, among others!

The objective of using AdWords to position advertisements on Google is to consider both the person's intent and their interests (based on the "keywords" they are using to search).In PPC, intent is a crucial factor, as it indicates whether a user is conducting research or purchasing.

If they want to learn more, they may look up "top computer games this year," and if they want to purchase something, they may look up the name of the computer game or what are commonly referred to as "cheap video games." Additionally, you can use "negative keywords" to eliminate words and phrases (such as "free download") that may indicate that a consumer is uninterested in making a purchase and, therefore, has the wrong intent.

PPC aims to ensure that only individuals who are likely to make a purchase from you select the link. This decreases expenditures while increasing prospective earnings. This necessitates that advertisements be "targeted" to the appropriate audience as precisely as possible, even if it means discouraging potential consumers with the appropriate content.

Obviously, the link should lead users to a sales page so that you can increase your revenue. You should then concentrate on the site's conversion rate. In other terms, 1% of visitors may convert if your landing page is well-written (i.e., 1% of visitors may make a purchase). If you increase this sum, you will be able to spend more on advertising while still turning a profit.

Chapter 12: Covers Audience Growth And Product Marketing

For example, a "fitness" website is too generic and hackneyed to be popular. It requires competing with the entire internet. How do you distinguish yourself in such a competitive market?

Consider creating a website about fitness for individuals over the age of 40. Instead, consider Paleo Fitness. Additionally CrossFit. Alternatively, you can exercise outside. Alternatively, Extreme Bodybuilding.

All of these alternatives have a more specific target audience, a more specific mission statement, and a more engaging appeal. Each will appeal to a smaller number of people, but those who are interested will be MUCH more likely to engage and be ecstatic that something is available just for them.

The brand should then emanate from this clear and genuine purpose. This implies that a person should be able to immediately determine whether they like your logo or website layout simply by glancing at it. Your brand should explicitly communicate who it is for and what it stands for, and your content should reinforce this message.

The website for serious bodybuilders will likely be red and black, with numerous articles on "raising testosterone with compound lifts" and sinister images of incredibly powerful men.

On the other hand, the paleo fitness website will likely be green and white with images of individuals running outdoors. From this point forward, your marketing, social media posts, and EVERYTHING else should be consistent with this impression.

Then, when you select your affiliate product, it should preferably target the same market. In addition, you will sell and promote the product using this value proposition.

Additionally, it is essential that you provide fresh, original content that demonstrates genuine expertise.

If you engage a writer who is unfamiliar with the subject, you will NEVER sell the affiliate product. Why?

Given this, the only option for the paid writer is to research the topic and restate it in their own words.

This means that none of the information will be new or intriguing, and it may even be out-of-date or inaccurate (since they won't be familiar enough with the topic to know when this is the case).

Find a writer with genuine interest in the topic, or compose it yourself. Why? Because they will then have something NEW and intriguing to say! This is how you establish yourself as a thought leader and convince others to join your mailing list and follow you by listening to you.

Be bold. Be different. Exhibit enthusiasm. Choose a product that appeals to that market.

Don't have time for that? Here are the options that are available to you.

Setting up Your Link

As an affiliate marketer, selling is incredibly simple. You are given one link to promote a product, from which you can generate sales and revenue regardless of where you position it. The dilemma then becomes: where do you place it?

The vast majority of us will position our link on a landing page or sales page, but this is just one option. In this section, we will examine how that functions, along with a number of other options.

Building a Sales Page

A website's sales page is a page designed with the sole purpose of generating revenue. This means that it will not provide any additional content (such as articles), links, or advertisements. Anything that could potentially detract attention from the product you are selling should be absent.

Typically, a sales page will have a long and narrow layout, which will encourage users to continue perusing and spend more time reading your content. They will feel like a waste of time if they depart without making a purchase, which will make it much more difficult for them to make a purchase!

However, writing is most important. Summarize your sales If your presentation is effective, this captive audience may be converted into ardent customers.

You can become a marketing Jedi by utilizing the incredibly effective strategy of persuasive writing. You do not seek out these drones.

Ultimately, you will be much more successful at making sales, attracting subscribers to your list, and achieving any other objective if you know how to persuade an audience with words.

Then, what actions are required to obtain this superpower? The accompanying guidance will prove useful.

People have limited time to peruse lengthy passages of text. If you want to persuade your audience, you must first get them to read what you have to say. Why do you do this? A strategy is to begin strongly. Using a narrative format is a further method for engaging the audience. Obviously, it is difficult for us to cease reading a novel before its conclusion, so the latter is very effective.

People will not always trust you because they do not know you and they are aware that you are attempting to sell them something. Let the numbers speak for themselves. Your argument will become more convincing as you cite more facts and authorities.

Anticipate: Attempt to anticipate the concerns that your readers will have so that you can address them promptly. You may, for example, mention that there are "many fantastic-sounding offerings online," but you must emphasize that this is not "just another hoax."

Reduce risk: people have a natural tendency toward "loss aversion." This indicates that they prefer to retain their current possessions over acquiring new ones. Then, you must eliminate all risk factors by offering money-back guarantees and trial periods without risk.

Understanding the value proposition is of vital importance. The promise that your product will improve the lives of your consumers is what gives it emotional significance. You should be aware that you are not, for example, selling a fitness-related eBook if you are selling one.

You are selling the sensation of having boundless vitality, six-pack abs, and abundant confidence. You must prioritize this! Try to evoke emotion in the reader by speaking from the heart, preferably enthusiasm for purchasing your product.

Keep in mind that many digital products will include comparable pre-made sales pages, so you can simply copy and paste the script onto your own page.

Now that you have a sales page, you only need to direct your audience there to begin generating conversions. Emails and social media platforms can be utilized for this purpose. You can even position product advertisements in the sidebar of your website and in other locations.

Chapter 13: Utilizing And Various Other Platforms For Direct Sales

Obviously, you can also sell directly through these other sites. There is nothing preventing you from posting an affiliate link to your Instagram or Facebook group (in your profile, or once the swipe up feature is available on stories). If you lack the time or resources to create a website, this is a useful strategy for attracting an interested audience.

You now have all the information necessary to establish a highly successful affiliate marketing business. You decide whether to keep things simple or to shoot for the stars, but I strongly advise you to follow the advice in this book and sell physical products with broad appeal and high prices in addition to digital eBooks and courses.

The conventional approach to marketing affiliate products is simple:

• Research digital products and acquire an affiliate link.

• Construct a sales page.

• Include a link to the product page.

• Drive traffic to the purchases page from your own website and marketing efforts.

- Utilize the product until sales cease, and then repeat.

To increase your earnings, I recommend modifying this model minimally.

Here is the revised strategy:

- Create a website and attract an audience that respects and values your work.

To accomplish this, you must produce content that is genuinely original and driven by an enticing visual identity and mission statement.

- Develop sales pages for a handful of high-priced affiliate products and services, then "launch" them from your website using email blasts and teasers to generate interest.

Determine the most popular products, and then use paid advertising to attract additional consumers. Use SEO-promoted articles and websites to sell as many lesser digital products, Amazon physical products, and services as possible in the interim.

Regardless of your preferences, you can now earn money while you slumber. The more attempts you make, the more efficient you become.

The Best-Kept Affiliate Marketing Secrets!

Then, what enables a phenomenal affiliate to earn hundreds or thousands of sales when you can scarcely sell five units of the same product? Why do successful affiliates make so much more money than you?

Consider the following: both of you are selling the same product. The only thing that could be different is the marketing strategy. Below are some strategies you can employ to sell more like excellent affiliates. Consider including them in your strategy.

First strategy: adopt an extended view.

Without exception, super affiliates almost always have access to a substantial captive audience. As opposed to scrambling to find consumers whenever a new product goes live, they typically have these customers well in advance and pre-sell to them throughout the entire period leading up to the product launch.

On the other hand, ineffective affiliate marketers frequently employ a Google Cash-style strategy for all their endeavors.

When a new product launch is imminent, they will create a promotional website and use solitary ads or pay-per-click search engine ads to attract visitors.

However, this strategy has a significant drawback: consumers will almost always purchase a "big launch" product from an Internet marketer they are already familiar with.

You must therefore have a long-term strategy. Instead of focusing on each launch individually, plan a strategy that will be consistently effective over time. Create a list first, and then direct EVERY visitor to it. If you want to increase your sales, you should follow in the footsteps of outstanding affiliates.

The second tactic is to consistently pilfer from Super Affiliates.

Numerous prominent Internet marketers are also exceptional affiliates. You are able to observe their public personas with relative ease. It is possible to locate forum users. Visit their blogs if you wish. Additionally, you can sign up for their email listings. You can discover which websites they manage.

I recommend that you pay close attention to a select group of stellar affiliates and unwittingly adopt every lesson they offer. Join their mailing list and keep a watch out for when they begin selling items in advance. You can also discover how they avoid pre-sales and only discuss products a few days after they go on sale.

Super affiliates employ dozens of distinct techniques. Despite the fact that none of these strategies are necessarily "best," you can still benefit from each one because a stellar affiliate's use of them indicates their efficacy.

Third strategy: Ignore verbal communication and look for revealed preferences

chatter is nothing but chatter. Many Internet marketers will discuss a variety of income-generating opportunities. They will advise you to build a mailing list, utilize Google AdWords for advertising, and create viral content.

I would advise you to disregard what they say and focus on what they do, despite the fact that some of this information may be accurate and advantageous. This is known as "revealed preference." If something is effective, they will likely continue to use it, so keep an eye out for it and ignore the discussion.

Develop a rapport with the vendor (Strategy 4)

Surprisingly, the merchant desires your success as well. Get in touch with him beforehand, make him your acquaintance, and ask him for specific advice on how to sell the product.

Remember that he frequently communicates with numerous affiliates (especially during significant product launches) and has the most in-depth understanding of the strategies they employ.

Conclusion

In order to consistently outperform other affiliates in their niche, super affiliates employ a variety of strategies. However, they always play the long game. Prior to the release of new products, they create mailing lists, launch online communities, and secure a captive audience.

Chapter 14: Choosing The Appropriate Affiliate Program

The popularity of affiliate marketing programs has exploded in recent years. This trend is attracting millions of people because it is one of the quickest and easiest ways to launch a successful internet business from home. Affiliate networks enable businesses to employ vast armies of marketers who are compensated based on their success. Affiliates who are proficient in affiliate marketing can make thousands of dollars per month. As a result of this arrangement, the number of affiliate marketing programs has skyrocketed. In tandem with this expansion of affiliate opportunities, however, a slew of questions have arisen, such as "How do you go about selecting the most suitable affiliate program for your needs?" How can you determine if a program has everything you need to begin earning a living wage, and what features should you search for? Here are some considerations to make when evaluating affiliate programs in order to save time and money.

How much are affiliates paid for each sale?

Knowing the profit potential of a transaction is crucial. It is not worthwhile to advertise a product if the commissions are insignificant. It is possible for your marketing costs to exceed your sales revenue. Unless you have discovered a niche market where you can sell massive quantities of product and earn substantial commissions on your sales volume, you should likely adhere to marketing products with a high commission value.

How many visitors do they receive monthly?

Determine how much current traffic the affiliate owner's website receives. Alexa.com is an excellent tool for this type of research. If the website's Alexa traffic rank is greater than 100,000, the merchant likely receives a large number of visitors; consequently, the number of affiliates promoting the business may be saturated. It may be ineffective if it has a ranking below 500,000, or it may be an exceptional opportunity to profit as one of the first affiliates. Before making a purchase from a vendor with a low traffic rating, it is prudent to conduct additional research. If you have the means to do so, it may be preferable to purchase the product on your own. If you are still unsure, a quick Internet search should disclose whether or not it has received negative feedback. You should be wary of the advice you receive from individuals who continually complain about affiliate programs without providing any supporting evidence. A good rule of thumb is to avoid affiliate programs with numerous negative reviews and few positive reviews.

When are affiliates compensated for their work?

Some affiliate programs pay commissions weekly, others once a month, and still others every three months. If you want to be in control of your company's finances, you must know how frequently you will be paid. Is it possible for you to continue marketing a product if you won't be paid for an extended period? You should also discover the minimum commission amount that must be paid.

Are cookies utilized for tracking in the affiliate program?

First-time visitors to a retailer's website frequently depart without making a purchase. Therefore, it is essential that the merchant's affiliate program utilizes cookies, so that you receive credit when a customer makes a subsequent purchase. Determine how long the biscuits remain edible. The longer the cookies last, the greater your likelihood of receiving payment.

Does the Affiliate Program Offer Future Purchase Commissions?

Some affiliate networks only track purchases made by customers who followed a link from your site. If a consumer bypasses your site and proceeds directly to the merchant's, you will not receive a commission on any purchases made by that consumer. If you want to build a sustainable affiliate business, you must be compensated regardless of the channel through which the customer returns.

What type of marketing materials does the Affiliate Program offer?

Confirm the range and caliber of their marketing materials. Do they provide you with articles, advertisements, or anything else for your website? Are you able to provide your mailing list subscribers with free instructions, discounts, viral e-books, or product samples? Affiliates may presume that the company will treat them well if they receive high-quality promotional materials. It may be difficult to select the affiliate program that best meets your requirements. Do your own research, consider the information presented here, and rely on your intuition. Using the above queries, you can locate an affiliate program that will contribute to your financial success. Affiliate marketing is a risky endeavor, but you never know when you will strike it wealthy.

Conclusion:

Affiliate marketing is so popular because it does not require a conventional advertising budget. Nonetheless, this absence of financial investment may result in a lack of accountability among content marketers. This can encourage individuals to utilize affiliate marketing, which may be more accessible and less costly than traditional advertising channels.

Affiliate marketing is ideally suited for businesses that want to investigate new methods of acquiring traffic without making a financial or time commitment.

www.ingramcontent.com/pod-product-compliance
Lightning Source LLC
Chambersburg PA
CBHW050419120526
44590CB00015B/2033